One For You &

One For Me

Desserts for Humans and Dogs

Pumpkin Publishing
Naperville

First Edition

ISBN-13: 978-0615697673
ISBN-10: 0615697674

Pumpkin Publishing
Naperville

One For You & One For Me is dedicated to my family and friends who have encouraged me to start and finish writing my first cookbook.

A paws up to Kipper, who was always there to taste-test a recipe... over and over again.

A special hug to my editors: Jeff, my husband, and Hannah, my daughter.

Also, in remembrance to Wrigley and Baby. There will always be one for each of you.

CONTENTS

INTRODUCTION

Welcome to the sweet, savory, and scrumptious world of One For You & One For Me.

A world where you can bake delectable desserts not only for yourself, but also to share with your furry friend.

All of these yummy recipes can be quickly and easily executed. No complicated equipment or special baking skills are needed to whip up these goodies.

Be it a tart, cupcake, or cookie, sharing what you bake with your furry friend will bring delight to both of your worlds.

Dogs and humans, need to limit their sugar. Please monitor your dog's sugar intake. These desserts are meant for special treat times. I highly recommend using the mini donut or cupcake pans for your dogs desserts. This will help in serving portion reduction.

None of these recipes contain dairy. Dairy is hard for dogs to digest, and can cause stomach upset. In lieu of dairy you can use soy or coconut products. For example: instead of milk, the recipe will call for unsweetened coconut milk. For heavy cream, you can use an unsweetened soy creamer. Instead of using eggs, you can use unsweetened plain soy yogurt.

Since all the recipes call for a dairy replacement, I have include recommendations for certain brands that I believe are of the highest quality.

I also suggest using organic ingredients when at all possible. For example: your soy products, peanut butter, coconut milk, applesauce, pumpkin, carob, and bananas.

Flaxseed is needed in a few of the recipes. This may be a new ingredient for you. Flaxseed is high in Omega-3, and can be used as an egg replacement in certain recipes. One tablespoon of ground flaxseed is equivalent to 1 egg. For every tablespoon of flaxseed, you will need 3 tablespoons of warm water. Soak the flaxseed in the warm water for a few minutes until it gels.

Human foods you need to avoid giving your dog:

Avocado	Moldy Foods
Alcohol	Nutmeg
Chocolate	Onions
Coffee	Raisins
Garlic	Salt
Grapes	Tea
Macadamia Nuts	Walnuts
Dairy products	Xylitol
Mushrooms	Yeast

Sources: The Humane Society and the ASPCA

Human foods that are safe for your dog:

Carrots	Strawberries
Flaxseed	Bananas
Pumpkin	Carob
Apples	Raspberries
Oatmeal	Blueberries
Peanut butter	Coconut

The above list of safe foods was compiled from various sources.

Brands that I recommend using in these recipes:

- Earth Balance Vegan Buttery Sticks
- Spectrum Organic All Vegetable Butter Flavor Shortening
- Follow Your Heart Vegan Gourmet Sour Cream
- Daiya Cheddar Style Shreds & Cheddar Style Wedge
- Galaxy Nutritional Foods Vegan Classic Plain Cream Cheese Alternative
- WholeSoy & Co. Unsweetened Plain Organic Soy Yogurt
- SO Delicious Dairy Free Original Coconut Milk Creamer
- SO Delicious Unsweetened Dairy Free Coconut Milk
- Tempeh Smoky Maple Bacon
- Spectrum Essentials Organic Ground Premium Flaxseed
- Annie's Naturals Organic Worcestershire Sauce

Cakes

- Chocolate Covered Banana

- Banana Cinnamon Streusel

- Victorian Sponge

- Coconut Carob

- Banana Coconut Cream Layer

Chocolate Covered Banana Cake

Makes one 9" loaf

2/3 cup of non-dairy butter flavored shortening
2 cups unbleached flour
1 cup organic sugar
1 1/4 teaspoons baking powder
1 teaspoon baking soda
1 1/2 cups mashed organic bananas
2/3 cup organic coconut milk
2 tablespoons organic flaxseed soaked in 6 tablespoons of warm water

Carob Frosting

6 ounces organic carob chips
1/4 cup organic coconut creamer

Preheat oven to 350°F

Grease a 9" loaf pan with the non-dairy shortening, set aside.

In a large bowl, blend the shortening and all of the dry ingredients together. Add the mashed bananas, coconut milk, and flaxseed mixture. Mix thoroughly.

Pour the batter into the greased loaf pan and bake for 35 minutes.

Making the carob frosting

Place the coconut creamer and carob chips in a double boiler or a microwave-safe bowl. Remove when the carob is completely melted and mixture is smooth.

Let the frosting cool completely before using.

Remove the cooled banana cake from the loaf pan. Slice a piece for you, and a smaller piece for your furry friend. Add a dollop of the carob frosting on top.

Enjoy!

Banana Cinnamon Streusel

Cake Batter

2 cups unbleached flour
1 teaspoon baking powder
1/2 teaspoon baking soda
3/4 cup organic sugar
1 stick non-dairy butter, plus roughly 1
tablespoon to grease loaf pan
3 ripe organic bananas (mashed very well)
1 teaspoon pure vanilla extract
1 tablespoon organic ground flaxseed
(mixed with 3 tablespoons of warm water)

Streusel Topping

5 tablespoons unbleached flour
3 tablespoons non-dairy butter, softened
1 teaspoon cinnamon

Preheat oven to 350°F

Lightly coat a 5x3 loaf pan with butter and then with flour. Set aside.

Making the streusel

In a small bowl, combine the flour, butter, and cinnamon together with a fork until a crumbly mixture forms. Set aside.

Making the cake

In a medium bowl, combine the flour, baking powder, and baking soda. Set aside.

In a separate bowl, beat the butter and sugar until creamy with either a stand mixer or a hand-held mixer. Add the flaxseed mixture, mashed bananas, and vanilla. Beat until well-combined. Lastly, add the flour mixture and beat until well-incorporated.

Spoon the batter into the prepared loaf pan. Sprinkle the streusel topping evenly over the batter.

Bake the cake for 40-50 minutes.

Remove from oven and let cool for 15 minutes before moving from pan to cake plate.

Victorian Sponge Cake

This is the perfect birthday cake! Blow up
those balloons and celebrate!

Cake Batter for two 9" round cakes

1 cup unsweetened organic coconut milk
1 teaspoon apple cider vinegar
2 tablespoons cornstarch
1 1/4 cups unbleached flour
3/4 teaspoon baking powder
1/2 teaspoon baking soda
1 teaspoon pure almond extract
1/3 cup oil
3/4 cup organic sugar
2 teaspoons pure vanilla extract
Non-dairy butter to grease cake pans

Coconut Whipped Cream Filling

Two 14 ounce cans of organic coconut milk,
chilled overnight
1 tablespoon pure vanilla extract
1/3 cup organic powdered sugar

Fruit Filling

4 tablespoons of sugar-free organic jam.
Try: apple, blueberry, raspberry, or
strawberry

Preheat oven to 350°F

Lightly grease two 9" round cake pans with
butter. Set aside.

Whisk coconut milk and vinegar together,
set aside for a few minutes to curdle.

In a medium-sized bowl combine corn starch, unbleached flour, baking powder, and baking soda. Set aside.

In a large bowl, beat together the coconut milk mixture, almond extract, oil, sugar, and vanilla extract. To that gradually add the flour mixture and combine well.

Pour the batter into the 2 greased cake pans.

Bake for 20 minutes, or until a toothpick comes out clean when inserted in the middle of both cakes. Let cakes cool before removing and adding whipped cream and filling.

While cakes are cooling, make the whipped cream.

Open the 2 cans of chilled coconut milk. Carefully scoop out the top thick layer of coconut milk, discard the liquid underneath. Or, you can save the liquid and drink it later. Place the thickened coconut milk in your mixer and add the vanilla and powdered sugar. Whisk until smooth, making sure not to over-mix, because doing so will deflate the whipped cream.

Place one cooled cake layer on a plate and spread the whipped cream evenly. On the second layer, spread the jam. Sandwich pieces together.

Let the party begin!

Coconut Carob Cake

Recipe yields one 9" cake

1/4 cup unsweetened organic non-dairy
plain yogurt
1/3 cup mashed organic banana
1/2 cup non-dairy butter, softened
1 1/4 cups unsweetened organic
coconut milk
2 teaspoons pure vanilla extract
1 1/2 cups unbleached flour
3/4 cup organic carob powder
1 teaspoon baking soda
2 teaspoons baking powder
1 cup organic flaked coconut

Preheat oven to 350°F

Place yogurt in a large bowl and mix in the mashed banana, butter, and coconut milk until creamy. Add the vanilla, flour, carob powder, baking soda, and baking powder. Combine thoroughly and stir in the flaked coconut.

Pour batter into a greased 9" round cake pan.

Bake for 20-25 minutes.

Cool before cutting or frosting.

Topping suggestions:
Sprinkle extra coconut on top
White Chocolate Sour Cream Frosting
Coconut Whipped Cream

Banana Coconut Cream Layer Cake

Cake Batter for two 9" round cakes

1/2 cup non-dairy butter flavored
shortening, plus more to grease cake pans
1/2 cup organic sugar
2 1/4 cups unbleached flour
1/2 teaspoon baking soda
2 1/2 teaspoons baking powder
3/4 cup unsweetened organic plain
non-dairy yogurt
1 1/2 teaspoons pure vanilla extract
1/4 cup unsweetened organic coconut milk
1 cup mashed organic bananas

Preheat oven to 350°F

Cream shortening and sugar until fluffy in a stand mixer or with a hand-held mixer. Add the flour, baking soda, and baking powder. To that add the yogurt and vanilla. Blend until well-combined.

Add the milk and mashed bananas. Do not over mix.

Divide the batter into two greased 9" round cake pans.

Bake for 25-30 minutes.

Coconut Cream Filling

Two 14 ounce cans of organic coconut milk, chilled overnight
1 tablespoon pure vanilla extract
1/3 cup organic powdered sugar

While the cakes are baking, make the Coconut Cream Filling.

In the bowl of a stand mixer or with a hand-held mixer, attach the whisk. Open both cans of coconut milk and carefully remove the thick top layer and place in bowl. Refrigerate the remaining liquid to drink later. Add the vanilla extract and powdered sugar. Whisk until well-combined. Do not over beat or you will deflate the cream. Refrigerate for 2 hours before using. This will thicken the whipped cream.

Once the cakes have cooled, place one cake on a large round plate. This will be your bottom layer. Spread the coconut whipped cream evenly over cake. Place 2nd layer on top.

Topping suggestion: Lightly toast coconut flakes in a 300°F oven for 20 minutes. Stir every 5 minutes so the coconut browns evenly. Sprinkle evenly over the top layer.

Cookies

- Tom Thumb Cookies with Fruit Filling

- Barb's Kolachkies

- Carob Bonbon Cookies

- Shortbread Fudge Buttons

- Banana Cookies with Peanut Butter Frosting

Tom Thumb Cookies with Fruit Filling

Recipe yields 2 dozen cookies

3/4 cup butter flavored non-dairy
shortening
1/2 cup organic light brown sugar
1/2 cup organic unsweetened peanut butter
1 3/4 cups unbleached flour
1 teaspoon pure vanilla extract
1 tablespoon flaxseed, soaked in 3
tablespoons warm water
1 jar of organic sugar free jelly
(your flavor choice)

Preheat oven to 350°F

Line baking sheets with parchment paper,
set aside.

Cream shortening and brown sugar until
smooth. Blend in peanut butter, flaxseed,
vanilla, and flour.

Shape into 1 inch balls, make a deep well in
the center of each cookie with your thumb,
or paw.

Bake for 12-15 minutes.

Remove from oven and let cookies cool on a
cooling rack. Fill centers with your choice
of jelly.

Barb's Kolachkies

Recipe yields 2 1/2 dozen cookies

8 oz. non-dairy butter
8 oz. non-dairy cream cheese
2 cups unbleached flour
2 teaspoons baking powder
3/4 cup organic powdered sugar
Unsweetened organic apple, strawberry,
raspberry or blueberry jelly/jam for the
filling

Preheat oven to 350°F

Line baking sheets with parchment paper, set aside.

Cream butter and cream cheese together until smooth. Add flour, baking powder, and powdered sugar. Blend thoroughly.

Form dough into two 2" diameter rolls, wrap in plastic wrap and refrigerate for 1 hour.

Slice each roll into 1/2" slices, place on cookie sheets. Make thumbprint or paw print in the center of each slice and fill with fruit filling.

Bake for 15 minutes.

Remove from oven and let cool completely before enjoying.

Carob Bonbon Cookies

Recipe yields 1 1/2 dozen cookies

1/2 cup non-dairy butter, softened
3/4 cup organic confectioners sugar
1 tablespoon pure vanilla extract
1 1/2 cups unbleached flour
1-2 tablespoons of unsweetened
organic coconut milk, if needed
Organic carob chips

Frosting (optional)

1 cup creamy organic no sugar peanut
butter
(If your peanut butter is in the refrigerator,
remove and let sit 20 minutes to soften.)

Preheat oven to 300°F

Blend butter, sugar, and vanilla in a
medium-size mixing bowl. Mix in flour until
thoroughly combined. If the dough seems
to be dry, you can add 1 to 2 tablespoons
of coconut milk.

Take a heaping tablespoon of dough and
mold around a few pieces of carob chips,
forming a ball. Place cookies 1 inch apart on
a parchment-lined baking sheet.

Bake 12 to 15 minutes. Do not let the
bonbons brown. Remove from baking sheet
and let cool on wire rack.

Using a teaspoon or a pastry bag, place a
small dollop of peanut butter on top of
each bonbon.

Shortbread Fudge Buttons

Recipe yields 2 dozen cookies

1 cup butter flavored non-dairy shortening
2/3 cup organic sugar
2 teaspoons pure vanilla extract
2 cups unbleached flour
1/4 cup cornstarch
1/4 cup unsweetened organic coconut milk

Carob Fudge Filling

4 ounces organic carob chips
1/4 cup organic coconut creamer
1 tablespoon organic agave nectar

Preheat oven to 350°F

Line your cookies sheets with parchment paper and set aside.

Beat the shortening, sugar, and vanilla until smooth.
Add the flour and cornstarch. When the mixture is well combined, add the coconut milk and beat until you form a soft dough.

Roll the dough into 1 inch balls, place on cookie sheets.
Using your thumb or paw, make a small well in each cookie.

Bake for 10-12 minutes. Remove from the oven and let cool on a wire rack.

Making the filling

In a medium saucepan over low heat, bring the coconut creamer and agave nectar to a gentle boil.

Remove from heat and stir in the carob chips. Stir until the chips have all melted into a smooth texture.

Let the filling cool before adding to the cookies.

Fill each cookie with the fudge mixture.

Aren't they cute as a button?

Banana Cookies with Peanut Butter Frosting

Recipe yields 2 dozen cookies

1 very ripe organic banana
1 teaspoon pure vanilla extract
1/2 cup organic sugar
1/4 cup oil
3/4 unbleached flour
1/2 teaspoon baking soda
1 teaspoon cinnamon
1 1/2 cups quick cooking organic oatmeal

Peanut Butter Frosting

4 tablespoons non-dairy butter, softened
1/4 cup organic confectioners sugar
3/4 cup organic unsweetened creamy
 peanut butter

Preheat oven to 350°F

Line 2 baking sheets with parchment paper, set aside.

In a large mixing bowl, mash the banana, and add vanilla, sugar, and oil mix until well combined. To that add flour, baking soda, cinnamon, and lastly, the oats.

Roll dough into small paw-size balls. Place cookies a couple of inches apart on the cookie sheets.

Bake for 10-12 minutes, or until lightly browned. Let cookies cool before frosting.

While cookies are cooling, and your furry family member is camped out in front of the smell of yummy goodness, make the frosting.

Mix the butter, sugar and peanut butter in a medium sized bowl until smooth.

Frost cookies.

Lastly, sit down with your furry camper and enjoy a cookie, or two.

Cupcakes

- Orange Pumpkin Cupcakes

- Banana Coconut Cupcakes

- Peanut Butter Cupcakes

- Brownie Cupcakes with Buttercream Frosting

Orange Pumpkin Cupcakes

Recipe yields 5 large cupcakes and
8 mini cupcakes

2 cups unbleached flour
1 teaspoon baking powder
1/2 teaspoon baking soda
1/3 cup unsweetened organic applesauce
1 1/2 teaspoons cinnamon
1/2 teaspoon pure vanilla extract
1/2 cup orange juice
1/2 cup organic canned pumpkin
1 tablespoon ground organic flaxseed,
soaked in 3 tablespoons of warm water

Preheat oven to 350° F

Combine the flour, baking powder, baking soda, applesauce, and cinnamon in a large bowl. Add the pumpkin, flaxseed mixture, vanilla extract, and orange juice. Mix until smooth and well-combined.

Fill each cupcake wrapper two-thirds full. Bake for 35-40 minutes.

These cupcakes can be enjoyed plain, or you may frost them using the white chocolate sour cream frosting.

*Remember, use the mini cupcake pan for your furry family member's cupcakes.

Banana Coconut Cupcakes

Recipe yields 5 large cupcakes and
8 mini cupcakes

1/3 cup butter flavored non-dairy
shortening
2/3 cup unsweetened organic coconut milk
2 very ripe organic bananas, mashed
3/4 cup unsweetened organic non-dairy
plain yogurt
3/4 cup organic unsweetened applesauce
2 1/2 cups unbleached flour
1 1/4 teaspoons baking powder
1 teaspoon baking soda
1 cup organic carob chips, optional

Preheat oven to 350°F

In a large bowl, combine shortening, coconut milk, mashed bananas, yogurt, and applesauce. Beat in the flour, baking powder, and baking soda. At this point you can add a cup of carob chips if desired.

Fill each cupcake liner two-thirds full. Bake for 35 minutes, or until a toothpick comes out clean when inserted into the center of each cupcake.

You can enjoy these cupcakes with or without frosting.

*Remember, use the mini cupcake pan for your furry family member.

Peanut Butter Cupcakes

Recipe yields 5 large cupcakes, and
8 mini cupcakes

2 cups unbleached flour
2 1/2 teaspoons baking powder
2 teaspoons cinnamon
1/2 cup organic brown sugar
1/3 cup buttered flavored non-dairy
shortening
1 1/2 teaspoons pure vanilla extract
3/4 cup unsweetened organic coconut milk
1/2 cup unsweetened organic peanut butter
3/4 cup unsweetened organic plain
non-dairy yogurt

Preheat oven to 350°F

In a medium-sized bowl, combine flour, baking powder, and cinnamon, set aside.

With a stand mixer or a hand-held mixer, cream the brown sugar, shortening, and vanilla until fluffy. Add peanut butter, continue mixing until well-combined, then add the yogurt.

Alternate adding the flour mixture and coconut milk to the creamed mixture. Mix until all ingredients are well-combined.

Fill each cupcake liner two-thirds full.

Bake for 25-30 minutes.

Let cool before enjoying or frosting.

*Remember to use the mini cupcake pan for your furry family member.

Any of the frosting recipes in this book will work well with these cupcakes.

Brownie Cupcakes with Buttercream Frosting

This batter will yield 6 cupcakes and 6 mini cupcakes.

2 cups unbleached bleached flour
1/2 cup organic sugar
1/4 cup organic carob powder
1 teaspoon baking powder
1 cup water
1/2 cup oil
1 teaspoon pure vanilla extract

Preheat oven to 350° F

In a large bowl combine the flour, sugar, carob powder, and baking powder. Add the water, oil, and vanilla. Stir until the batter is smooth.

Fill each cupcake liner 3/4 full. Bake for 20-25 minutes. The mini cupcakes will take less time to bake, check at 10-15 minutes.

Buttercream Frosting

1/4 cup non-dairy butter flavored shortening
1/2 cup non-dairy butter, softened
1 1/4 cup organic powdered sugar
3/4 teaspoon pure vanilla extract

In a medium bowl cream the shortening and butter. Add the sugar and vanilla. Continue beating until you have a thick smooth frosting.

Frost cupcakes when they are cool to the touch.

Donuts

- Mini Applesauce Donuts

- Carob Donuts

Mini Applesauce Donuts

1 cup unbleached flour
1 teaspoon baking soda
1 teaspoon baking powder
1 tablespoon cinnamon
1/2 cup unsweetened organic coconut milk
1/3 cup unsweetened organic
non-dairy creamer
1/2 cup organic unsweetened applesauce
1/2 teaspoon pure vanilla
Non-dairy butter to grease the donut pan

Preheat oven to 400°F

Grease mini-donut pan with butter, set
aside.

In a small bowl, combine flour, baking soda, and baking powder. Set aside.

In a large bowl, whisk together the coconut milk, creamer, applesauce, and vanilla.

Fold flour mixture into the wet ingredients and gently combine until moist.

Add 1 1/2 tablespoons of batter to each donut mold. Make sure to leave the center peg visible.

Bake for 10 minutes. Remove from oven, let stand for 2 minutes. Remove donuts, let cool before icing.

Use any of the glaze or frosting recipes in this book to top your donuts.

Carob Donuts

These donuts are baked, not fried. So the consistency will be dense, making it the perfect carrier for heavy glazes or frostings.
For this recipe you will need a donut pan. I do recommend the mini donut pan for your dog, this helps control calories. We don't want our dogs rolling around like a donut.

1/4 cup unsweetened organic plain non-dairy yogurt
1/2 cup organic sugar
1 teaspoon pure vanilla extract
1/2 cup unsweetened organic non-dairy creamer
1 cup unbleached flour
1 cup cake flour
1/4 cup organic carob powder
1/2 teaspoon baking soda
1 teaspoon baking powder
Non-dairy butter to grease donut pans

Preheat oven to 325°F

Lightly grease the pan(s) with the butter.

With a mixer, beat the yogurt and sugar until well-blended. Add vanilla and creamer, beat until mixture is smooth.

In a large bowl mix the flours, carob powder, baking soda, and baking powder.

Gradually add the dry mixture to the wet mixture, beating until well combined.

Refrigerate the dough for 20-30 minutes.

For the standard donut pan, you will want to take a heaping spoonful of dough and roll it between your hands to make a 4 inch long tube. Place the tube into the pan, meeting the two ends and pinching them closed.

Do the same for the mini donuts, reduce the amount of dough to a heaping teaspoon of dough.

Bake for 15 minutes, remove from oven, and let cool before frosting. Use any of the frostings or glazes in this book to customize your donut.

Frostings and Glazes

- White Chocolate
  Sour Cream Frosting

- Almond Frosting

- Vanilla Glaze

- Thick Vanilla Glaze

White Chocolate Sour Cream Frosting

12 ounces vegan white chocolate
1 1/2 cups non-dairy sour cream

Melt the white chocolate using a double boiler or a microwave until smooth and creamy. Remove and let chocolate cool. Stir in the sour cream.

Set the mixture aside for 2-3 hours to let thicken.

This frosting can be used on cupcakes, cakes, donuts, or even cookies.

Almond Frosting

1/4 cup non-dairy shortening
1/2 cup non-dairy butter
1 1/4 teaspoons pure almond extract
1/4 cup organic powdered sugar

Cream non-dairy shortening and butter
until well-combined. Add the almond
extract and powdered sugar. Beat into a
thick frosting.

*For a chocolate frosting, add 1/4 cup
organic carob powder.

Vanilla Glaze

5 tablespoons non-dairy butter, melted
2 cups organic confectioner's sugar
1 1/2 teaspoons pure vanilla extract
5 tablespoons hot water

In a medium bowl, whisk the melted butter with the confectioner's sugar and vanilla. Add the hot water and blend until smooth.

Transfer the glaze to a bowl with low sides and dip the top half of all the donuts into the glaze. Let the glazed donuts rest on a wire rack for 10 minutes before enjoying.

Thick Vanilla Glaze

2 cups organic confectioner's sugar
1 teaspoon organic light corn syrup
1 1/2 teaspoons pure vanilla extract
3 tablespoons hot water

In a medium bowl, whisk together the confectioner's sugar, corn syrup and vanilla. Add the hot water and whisk into a smooth glaze.

Transfer glaze to a bowl with low sides and dip the top half of all the donuts into the glaze. Let the glazed donuts rest on a wire rack for 10 minutes.

Ice Cream

- Banana Coconut Ice Cream

- Carob and Coconut Ice Cream

Banana Coconut Ice Cream

7 medium sized ripe organic bananas
3/4 cup organic agave nectar
1 1/2 teaspoons pure vanilla extract
One 13.5 fl. oz. can of unsweetened organic
coconut milk

Peel and slice the bananas into 1" chunks,
freeze overnight in a freezer bag. Remove
from freezer and let thaw 10 minutes before
making ice cream.

Place bananas into a blender with the agave
nectar and vanilla. Blend until smooth.

With the mixer running slowly, pour in the
coconut milk. Mix until smooth.

Pour mixture into your ice cream maker and
mix until you reach the consistency you
prefer. Remove and place ice cream into a
freezer-safe container.

If you're not using an ice cream maker, directly pour mixture into a freezer safe container.

Either way, freeze until firm.

Carob and Coconut Ice Cream

1 1/4 cups canned organic
unsweetened coconut milk
1/4 cup organic carob powder
1/4 cup organic agave nectar
1 tablespoon coconut oil
1/4 cup maple syrup

In a blender, combine all ingredients until
smooth. Pour into ice cream maker and
blend until you reach the consistency you
prefer, or directly place mixture into a
freezer safe container and freeze until firm.

Muffins

- Grandma Sandy's Bacon and Cheese Muffins

- Apple Banana Muffins with Banana Frosting

- Apple Cinnamon Muffins

Grandma Sandy's
Bacon and Cheese Muffins

Recipe yields 8 large muffins and
6 mini muffins

These muffins go great with a salad.

2 cups unbleached flour
1/4 cup organic sugar
3 teaspoons baking powder
1 cup organic soy milk
1/3 cup non-dairy butter flavored
shortening (melted)
1 tablespoon organic ground flaxseed,
soaked in 3 tablespoons warm water
1/2 cup bacon substitute strips
(approx. 7 strips needed)
1 cup shredded non-dairy cheddar cheese
1 teaspoon oil

Preheat oven to 400°F

In a large skillet, warm 1 teaspoon of oil. Chop the bacon substitute strips into small pieces. Add to the skillet and cook until crispy. Remove from heat and set aside.

In a medium bowl, combine all the dry ingredients.

In another medium bowl, combine all the wet ingredients.

Pour the wet mixture into the dry mixture and mix until combined. Add the bacon and cheese and mix well.

Fill muffin wrappers halfway.

Bake for 20-25 minutes.

Your furry friend will flip for these minis.

Apple Banana Muffins with Banana Frosting

Recipe yields 8 large muffins, and 12 mini cupcakes

1/3 cup butter flavored non-dairy shortening
1/2 cup organic sugar
2 cups whole wheat flour
1 1/4 teaspoons baking powder
2 teaspoons cinnamon
1/2 cup unsweetened organic applesauce
2 very ripe organic mashed bananas
2/3 cup unsweetened organic coconut milk
2 tablespoons flaxseed, blend into 6 tablespoons warm water

Banana Frosting

1/4 cup organic agave nectar
1 organic banana
3 tablespoons whole wheat flour

Preheat oven to 350°F

Beat shortening and sugar together until
well-combined. Add flour, baking powder,
and cinnamon. Stir well. Add applesauce,
mashed bananas, coconut milk, and
flaxseed mixture. Combine well.

Pour batter into muffin cups half-way full.

Bake for 30-35 minutes

In the meantime, let's make the frosting.

In a medium bowl, beat the agave with the banana, adding flour as needed to help set-up the frosting. Stop adding the flour when you have reached a consistency that you like.

Refrigerate until you're ready to frost the cooled muffins.

*Remember to use the mini cupcake pan for your furry family member.

Apple Cinnamon Muffins

Recipe yields 8 large muffins and
10 mini muffins

1/4 cup unsweetened organic plain
non-dairy yogurt
1/4 cup non-dairy butter, melted
2/3 cup organic sugar
1 tablespoon cinnamon
1 cup unsweetened organic coconut milk
1/2 teaspoon pure vanilla extract
2 cups unbleached flour
3 teaspoons baking powder
1 cup organic apple, peeled and chopped
Non-dairy butter to grease muffin pan

Preheat oven to 450°F

Beat the yogurt, butter, sugar, and cinnamon until smooth. Stir in coconut milk and vanilla. Mix in the flour and baking powder. Fold in apples.

Fill lightly greased muffin cups 2/3 full. Bake for 20 minutes.

*Remember to use the mini pans for your furry family member.

Tartlets

- Scrumptious Tartlets
  with Fruit Filling

- Petal Tartlets with Applesauce

- Delectable Cheese Tartlets

Scrumptious Tartlets
with Fruit Filling

Pastry dough for 24 mini tarts

3 ounces non-diary cream cheese, softened
1/2 cup non-dairy butter, softened
1 1/2 teaspoons pure almond extract
1 cup unbleached flour
1 jar of organic sugar-free fruit jam or jelly

With a mixer, blend cream cheese, butter,
and almond extract until smooth. Add flour
and beat until thoroughly incorporated.

Remove pastry mixture from bowl and place
on a sheet of plastic wrap. Form a disc and
chill in the refrigerator for 1 hour.

Preheat oven to 325°F

Press 1/2 tablespoon of pastry dough into each mini-muffin, making a shallow shell.

Bake the tartlets until they are a light golden brown.

Remove from pan and let cool.

Fill each tartlet with your choice of sugar-free organic jam or jelly.

Petal Tartlets with Applesauce

Recipe yields 2 dozen mini tartlets

1/2 cup butter flavored non-dairy
shortening
1/4 cup unsweetened organic plain
non-dairy yogurt
3/4 teaspoon pure vanilla extract
1/2 cup organic sugar
1 1/2 cups unbleached flour
1/4 teaspoon baking soda
Non-dairy shortening to grease
mini muffin pan

Mix shortening, yogurt, vanilla, and sugar in
a medium-sized bowl.

Add the flour and baking soda into the
blended shortening mixture. Mix
thoroughly.

Refrigerate dough several hours or overnight.

Preheat oven to 400°F

Roll the dough a half-inch thick on a lightly floured flat surface. Cut out the dough using a 3 inch rounded scalloped cookie cutter.

Gently place the rounds into a lightly-greased mini muffin pan. Fill each cup with a half a tablespoon of organic unsweetened applesauce.

Bake the tartlets for 12 minutes.

Thoroughly cool before enjoying.

Decadent Cheese Tartlets

Recipe yields 1 1/2 dozen mini tarts

Making the pastry

3 ounces non-dairy cream cheese, softened
1/2 cup non-dairy butter, softened
1 cup unbleached flour

Filling

Non-dairy cheese, your choice of flavor

With a mixer, blend cream cheese and
butter until smooth. Add flour and beat
until well-combined.

Remove pastry mixture from bowl and place
on a sheet of plastic wrap. Wrap the dough

and form into a disc. Chill in refrigerator for
1 hour.

Remove from refrigerator and preheat oven
to 325°F

Using an ungreased mini muffin pan, press
about 1 tablespoon of pastry dough into
each muffin cup, creating a well. Place a
half of a teaspoon of cheese into each well.

Bake for 15 minutes, or until cheese has
melted and pastry is a light golden brown.

Remove from pan and let cool thoroughly
before enjoying.

Assorted Treats

- Peanut Butter Oat Balls
- Carob Whoopie Pies with Peppermint Filling
- Carob Brownies
- Pup-kin Carob Chip Squares
- Cinnamon Teacakes
- Apple Cheese Bread
- Coconut Whipped Cream with Bananas
- Cheese Noms

Peanut Butter Oat Balls

1/2 cup unsweetened organic coconut milk
1 cup organic unsweetened peanut butter
3 cups rolled oats

Combine the coconut milk and peanut butter in a medium sized bowl. Stir in the rolled oats.

Roll the mixture into 1 inch balls, place on a parchment lined cookie sheet. Refrigerate for 1 hour.

Store in a tightly sealed container.

Carob Whoopie Pies
with Peppermint Cream Filling

If Kipper could talk, he would shout,
"whoopie!" for these chocolate peppermint
wonders.

Cake batter for 8 Whoopie Pies

1 cup unbleached flour
1/4 cup organic carob powder
1/2 teaspoon baking soda
1/2 cup organic light brown sugar
5 tablespoons non-dairy butter
1 teaspoon pure vanilla extract
1 tablespoon ground organic flaxseed,
mixed with 3 tablespoons warm water
1/3 cup organic unsweetened coconut milk
Non-dairy butter to grease the pan

Peppermint Cream Filling

1/2 cup non-dairy butter
1 1/2 cups organic powdered sugar
3 teaspoons pure peppermint extract
1 tablespoon organic unsweetened
coconut milk

Preheat oven to 325°F

Lightly grease and flour the whoopie pie
pan, set aside.

In a medium bowl whisk together flour,
carob powder, and baking soda. Set aside.

With a stand mixer or a hand-held mixer,
beat the brown sugar and butter until well-
combined. Scrape down the sides of the
bowl as needed. Add the vanilla and

flaxseed mixture. Continue mixing until smooth.

Start adding the flour mixture, alternating with the coconut milk. Thoroughly mix.

Fill each whoopie well with 1 1/2 tablespoons of batter. The batter should spread evenly in the well, if not, lightly tap the pan on the counter to distribute batter.

Bake for 8-10 minutes.

Let the cakes cool for a few minutes in the pan. Remove the pies and place on a wire rack to fully cool.

Making the filling

Cream the powdered sugar and butter together using a stand mixer or a hand-held mixer. Add the peppermint extract and coconut milk. The mixture should resemble a frosting. Add more milk if needed.

Assembly:

Spread a heaping tablespoon of the peppermint filling on the flat side of one whoopie cake. Then top with the domed side of another whoopie cake.

Relax and enjoy!

Carob Brownies

1 cup plus 1/2 tablespoon non-dairy butter, softened
3/4 cup organic unsweetened applesauce
3/4 cup organic unsweetened plain non-dairy yogurt
1 cup unbleached flour
1/4 cup organic carob powder
1 teaspoon pure vanilla extract

Preheat oven to 300°F

Melt butter in a small saucepan. Remove from heat and mix in the applesauce and yogurt. In a medium-sized bowl combine the flour and carob powder. Fold the wet mixture into the dry mixture, add vanilla, and mix well.

Pour into a greased 6"x9" pan.

Bake for 45 minutes.

Cool before eating.

If a frosting is desired, use the peppermint filling from the Whoopie Pie recipe. Spread a thin layer on the cooled brownies.

Pup-Kin Carob Chip Squares

2 sticks non-dairy butter, softened
1/4 cup organic sugar
1/4 cup organic unsweetened plain
non-dairy yogurt
2 teaspoons pure vanilla extract
1 cup organic pumpkin
2 cups whole wheat flour
2 teaspoons cinnamon
3/4 teaspoon ginger
1 teaspoon baking soda
8 ounces organic carob chips

Preheat oven to 350°F

Line a 9x13 inch baking pan with parchment
paper, leaving an over hang on all sides.

In a medium bowl, cream the butter and
sugar until smooth. Add the yogurt and

vanilla, beat until smooth. Beat in pumpkin, flour, baking soda, and spices. Fold in carob chips.

Pour batter into prepared pan. Bake for 35-40 minutes.

Let cool. Remove by lifting the parchment paper overhang and place on a large plate.

Enjoy with your pup.

Cinnamon Teacakes

Recipe yields 2 1/2 dozen teacakes

1 cup non-dairy butter, softened
1/2 cup organic confectioners sugar
1 1/2 teaspoons pure vanilla extract
2 1/4 cups unbleached flour
Cinnamon

Preheat oven to 400°F

Using a stand mixer or a hand held blender beat butter, sugar, and vanilla thoroughly. Add the flour and continue mixing until well-combined.

Form dough into 1 inch balls and place on a parchment-lined baking sheet. Bake for 10 to 12 minutes. Do not let cookies brown. While the cookies are still slightly warm, roll in cinnamon.

Apple Cheese Bread

Makes one loaf

1/2 cup non-dairy butter, softened
2/3 cup organic sugar
3/4 cup organic unsweetened plain
non-dairy yogurt
1 teaspoon baking powder
1/2 teaspoon baking soda
2 cups unbleached flour
1 cup organic unsweetened applesauce
1 cup shredded non-dairy cheddar cheese

Preheat oven to 350°F

Cream butter and sugar and add the
yogurt, baking powder, and baking soda.
Fold in the flour until well-blended and then
add the cheese. Stir in applesauce.

Pour batter into a well-greased loaf pan.

Bake for 1 hour.

Let cool thoroughly before enjoying.

Coconut Whipped Cream with Bananas

1 organic banana
1 cup coconut whipped cream
 (prepared ahead of time)

Slice banana into 1 inch rounds, then slice into quarters.

Place the coconut whipped cream in a medium bowl and gently fold in banana pieces. Do not over mix; you don't want to deflate the coconut cream.

This whipped cream can be enjoyed on cupcakes, muffins and cakes.

Cheese Noms

No dog can resist these!

Recipe yields 24 noms

1 1/2 cups unbleached flour
1/4 teaspoon dry mustard
1/2 teaspoon paprika
1/2 cup butter flavored non-dairy
shortening
1 cup shredded non-dairy cheddar cheese
1/2 teaspoon vegan worcestershire sauce
1/3 cup organic unsweetened non-dairy
creamer

In a medium bowl, combine flour, dry
mustard, and paprika. Cut in the
shortening and cheese using a fork until the
mixture forms small crumbles.

In a small bowl, add the cream and worcestershire sauce. Mix until well-combined. Add to the flour mixture and mix until the dough holds together. You can add more creamer 1 teaspoon at a time if needed.

Preheat oven to 425°F

Use a tablespoon of dough for a good sized nom, or use a teaspoon for snack size. Roll into a ball, and slightly flatten between both hands.

Place rounds onto a parchment lined cookie sheet. Bake for 10-12 minutes. Flip the noms after 5-6 minutes.

Aromatherapy

- Lavender Water

- Sweet Peppermint Spray

- Bug Repellent

- GinGe Spray

There are a number of essential oils that are beneficial to both human and dog.

They are as follows:

Lavender

Human benefits: Decreases anxiety and depression, skin problems, and insomnia.

Dog benefits: Antibacterial, anti-itch, nerve calming and skin irritations.

Chamomile, Roman

Human benefits: Anti-inflammatory

Dog benefits: Nerve calming, muscle pains.

Eucalyptus

Human benefits: Anti-inflammatory

Dog benefits: Anti-inflammatory

Geranium

Human benefits: Deodorant, anti-bacterial

Dog benefits: Anti-fungal, skin irritations

Ginger

Human benefits: Motion sickness, reduces pain and inflammation

Dog benefits: Motion sickness

Marjoram, Sweet

Human benefits: Anti-fungal, anxiety, natural disinfectant

Dog benefits: Antibacterial, calming

Peppermint

Human benefits: Helps elevate stress, keeps the skin healthy, energizes

Dog benefits: Stimulates circulation

Sweet Orange

Human benefits: Anti-depressant, anti - inflammatory

Dog benefits: calming, deodorizing

The following recipes using essential oils are meant to be used as sprays, for the body, on fabrics, or room fresheners. Never spray into human or dog eyes or mouth. Nor use the essential oils in the same manner. These sprays are only to be used topically, never orally.

Lavender Water

There are many wonderful uses for lavender water that you and your furry family member will thoroughly enjoy.

First the ingredients:

1 good handful of fresh lavender with stems
Organic Vodka
20 drops of Organic Lavender Essential Oil
1 glass jar with a lid, the jar should be able to hold the whole lavender flower (stems included)

Place the lavender flowers into the glass jar. The stems should be facing up. Fill the jar with the organic vodka, add the essential oil, and seal with the lid.

Place the jar on a sunny window sill for 3 weeks.

After the 3 weeks, open jar and gently remove the lavender by the stems all at once. Hold the lavender flower tips facing down into the jar, and give them a gentle squeeze to release the lavender water trapped in the flowers.

When done squeezing, you can put the discarded flowers/stems down your garbage disposal, giving your drain a wonderfully clean smell.

If you have some bits from the lavender in your water you can pour the water through a strainer to remove any sediment.

Pour your completed lavender water into a dark- colored glass spray bottle.
Now you are ready for the array of benefits that lavender water has to offer.

Spray your pillows, linens, and blankets as well as your furry family member's bed.
By doing this you are using the anti-bacterial benefits of lavender. Also, the scent will help

ease any anxiety and help calm you and your dog.

Use as an air freshener, and or as an ironing spray.

Store in a dark, cool place.

Sweet Peppermint Spray

An uplifting spray that can be used as an air freshener, body spray, or a spray for bed linens, furniture, and dog beds.

Supplies needed:

1 small amber or dark blue glass spray bottle
Distilled water
25 drops of Organic Sweet Marjoram Essential Oil
25 drops of Organic Sweet Orange Essential Oil
35 drops of Organic Peppermint Essential Oil

Add the essential oils to the bottle, fill with the distilled water. Replace bottle spray top and shake a few times.

Shake well before each use. Store in a dark, cool place.

Bug Repellent

Supplies needed:

Witch Hazel
Almond Oil
Organic Lavender Essential Oil
Organic Eucalyptus Essential Oil
Organic Peppermint Essential Oil
1 small amber or dark blue glass spray bottle

Pour 1 ounce each of the witch hazel and
almond oil into the spray bottle. To that add 25
drops each of the Eucalyptus and Lavender
essential oils. Lastly, add 15 drops of the
Peppermint essential oil.

Shake well before each use.

Do not spray near eyes and mouth of humans
or dogs.

Store in a dark, cool place.

GinGe Spray

Use this as a healing room-spray, when you and/or your dog are not feeling well.

Supplies needed:

Organic Vodka
Organic Ginger Essential Oil
Organic Geranium Essential Oil
1 small amber or dark blue glass spray bottle

Place 30 drops each of the Ginger and Geranium essential oils in the bottle. Pour in enough vodka to fill the bottle.

Shake well before each use.

Spray up into the air, avoiding eyes and mouth.

Store in a dark, cool place.

About The Author

Anna Jurik is a Certified Canine Massage Therapist. She enjoys baking for her husband Jeff, daughter Hannah, and their Basenji, Kipper.

Anna leads a lifestyle that encourages the protection and welfare of animals. She works hard to resolve many of the current issues that endanger dogs as well as our other animal friends.

The purpose of One For You and One For Me cookbook is to help strengthen the human animal bond.

Everyone loves eating a sweet, and it's twice as sweet when you share.

Made in the USA
Middletown, DE
15 October 2017